Side-Stepping the Rules:

Broken or Not

THE SENSITIVE MAN'S GUIDE FOR ESCAPING THE CLUTCHES OF THE WOMAN WHO THINKS SHE'S MRS. RIGHT

A Parody of a Parody by
EDWARD GALLUZZI

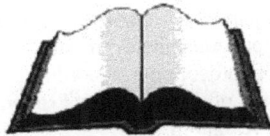

CCB Publishing
British Columbia, Canada

Side-Stepping the Rules: Broken or Not – The Sensitive Man's Guide for Escaping the Clutches of the Woman Who Thinks She's Mrs. Right

Copyright ©2010 by Edward Galluzzi
ISBN-13   978-1-926918-18-1
Third Edition

Library and Archives Canada Cataloguing in Publication
Galluzzi, Edward, 1951-
Side-stepping the rules : broken or not : the sensitive man's guide for
escaping the clutches of the woman who thinks she's Mrs. Right :
a parody of a parody / written by Edward Galluzzi – 3rd ed.
ISBN 978-1-926918-18-1
1. Man-woman relationships--Humor.
2. Dating (Social customs)--Humor. I. Title.
HQ801.G355 2010   646.7'70207   C2010-906455-0

United States Copyright Office Registration # TXu-853-074

Publisher: CCB Publishing
              British Columbia, Canada
              www.ccbpublishing.com

Dedication

I am dedicating this gift of laughter to my family…
my parents, Bill and Roberta; my sister Diane and her
family, Alan, Zachary and Nathan; my brother Rick and
his family, Sue and Michael; and my cousin Toni and
her family, Joe and Michael.

The few illustrations in this book are created and the
sole property of the author. They may not be repro-
duced, copied or transferred in any form. However, the
illustrations are so lame that the author would not even
consider prosecuting anyone who steals them 'cause he
does not have the time to challenge a legal insanity
defense.

Contents

Introduction

The reading of this introduction would be much more interesting and dynamic if you, the reader, would hum the theme from *Star Wars* as you read. OK? Ready?

Da, da, da, da—DA...

First, there was *The Rules: Time-tested Secrets for Capturing the Heart of Mr. Right* by Ellen Fein and Sherrie Schneider (Warner Books, 1995, ISBN: 0446602744). *The Rules* is presented as "a simple set of dos and don'ts" that will lead the reader to a "healthy, committed relationship." *The Rules* offers the female reader 35 rules to forge that path to a healthy relationship and includes the following: Be a creature unlike any other; Don't talk to a man first (and don't ask him to dance); Don't meet him halfway or go dutch on a date; Fill up your time before the date; Always end the date first; Don't live with a man (or leave your things in his apartment); and Do *The Rules even* when your friends and parents think it's nuts.

Da, da, da, da—DA...

Several years later came the parody book, *Breaking the Rules: Last-ditch Tactics for Landing the Man of Your Dreams* by Laura Banks and Janette Barber

(Career Press, 1997, ISBN: 0156442965). As a parody of *The Rules,* it offered, "All rules are made to be broken." The authors identify that *Breaking the Rules* women "don't give a damn." They offer 17 strategies in defining how such women engage men (so to speak) and include the following: Force yourself on men and tell them what they're thinking; Meet him anywhere and tell him where to go; Carry an answering machine in your purse; If he has a pulse, you have a date; Make your first date last at least 48 hours; Be at your best with PMS (needy, clingy and whiny); and Stay in your jammies and catch your man in Cyberspace.

Da, da, da, da—DA...

Now it is time for the *sensitive* man's point of view in this parody of a parody, *Side-Stepping the Rules: Broken or Not.* Unlike the previous two books, *The Rules* and *Breaking the Rules* (whose readings will help you understand and enjoy this book that much more), the parody *Side-Stepping the Rules: Broken or Not* offer men childish ways for escaping the clutches of the woman, even a *RB* (Rule Breakin') woman, who thinks she is *Mrs. Right.*

Da, da, da, da—DA...

Side-Stepping the Rules: Broken or Not provides the sensitive male with 11 manifestos that will serve as countermeasures to the wiles of *RB* women. No worries mate! If you fail to apply successfully the first manifesto, you still have 10 more chances to fight off those pesky *RB* women. Even if you are unsuccessful with the first 10 manifestos, the final manifesto, "Sell your house and blend invisibly with the homeless," still provides you, the most pitiful representation of *man*kind, a way out.

Da, da, da, da—DA...

For those readers who are inpatient and used cliff notes to progress through high school, save yourself time by turning to Chapter 12 now and *Consult Your MAN Index*. The *MAN Index* offers you the chance to pinpoint immediately how you will fare with the approach of a *RB* woman. The *MAN* Index is based grossly on an unscientific and nebulous study with the underlying theorem: You are what you eat!

Da, da, da, da—DA...

Finally, the reader is escorted or forced into the 21st century—depending on whether you now use an abacus or a computer. A glossary of terms is provided that help you understand women in Cyberspace. Don't enter the 21st century without it!

Da, da, da, da—DA...

OK. You can stop humming now...

WARNING: DO NOT SHOW THESE MANIFESTOS TO ANY WOMAN, ESPECIALLY *RB* WOMEN. SUCH A DIVULSION WILL COMPROMISE THESE COUNTERMEASURES AND MAKE YOU APPEAR MORE PATHETIC THAN YOU ARE. IF YOU BECOME IN DANGER OF BEING DISCOVERED OR THIS BOOK MIGHT BE REMOVED FROM YOUR POSSESSION, START EATING THESE PAGES NOW. BE A MAN AND SWALLOW IT. MASTICATION MAY BE YOUR ONLY SURVIVAL!

Manifesto 1

Shy Away From Women Who Show the Slightest Interest in You

Here is your chance: your chance to nip it, nip it, I say, nip it right in the bud! Women like to start something that most men can never finish. The male-female thing begins innocently enough: a female glance; a flitter; a dance; a jiggler. The male responds in a predictable manner: a return glance; a slither; a pant; a tickler. And now what?

Beware of women who initiate conversation—who initiate anything! If a woman asks you your hat size or shoe size, you know you are in trouble. The bane of *man*kind will certainly follow shortly! Can "What's your sign?" be that far off? Aries, Taurus, Gemini, Cancer, Leo, Virgo, Libra, Scorpio, Sagittarius, Capricorn, Aquarius or Pisces? It really doesn't matter which sign hovers over your head. Anyway, it's not your fault. You neither asked to be conceived between days embracing certain positions of heavenly bodies nor do you necessarily agree with a psychic's predictions of their influence on your affairs—even those prognostications by *professional* psychics.

Once a woman knows your astrological sign, however, your personality oozes out slowly like a melted molten mess of mucous membranes. You unintentionally spill your guts and what little self-control and self-determination you have as a man now runs amuck. Your little personality quirks are exposed, quirks that you have ardently and expertly kept hidden throughout your childhood, adolescence and most of your adult life—except, of course, from your mother and/or your psychotherapist if you are wealthy or well-insured.

You are cornered! When a woman begins attacking your personality flaws, you can only counter that without such flaws, you would have no personality at all! Ego, Igo, Ugo—it doesn't matter. If a woman shows the slightest interest in you, they all go! No matter how the conversation starts, it will always end the same way. So be weary of women who open a conversation. They can indeed be confusing.

Before the feminist movement, the ultimate goal of a woman's finagling was universal and twofold: get married and take care of your man (or was that stand by your man?). In the old days, this balanced well with the goal of man that was also universal and twofold: drink beer and watch sports. It was, as they say, a match made in heaven. Men and women were truly homo-sapiens. It was the stuff that bound us, the mortar between the sexes.

The feminist movement changed all that. Oh, do not misunderstand me. The goal of man is still the same, still the classic twofold: drink beer and watch sports. We are not particularly proud of it, but we men accept the fact that we are essentially one-dimensional. We have a narrow focus in life and have embraced such a focus without blinders. But women want something more out of life. They want a career. They want significance. They want equality. They want more than equality. They want dominance. In short, they want control. Women want to take that beer out of the hand of man and turn the television channel to *Ellen!* So women should no longer wonder why men never approach them; well, beyond the sex thing. Men have inalienable rights. Men who have encountered UFO's have alienable rights. It's no matter. Rights are rights. You're damn right: we'd rather be at home playing with our powerful power tools. We don't like women who force themselves on us, conversationally speaking. Men are basically shy, sensitive and gentle beings. It is hard for us to track a woman's conversational advances and simultaneously try to figure out what they are really saying. The male corpus callosum does not help bridge the gap. The Vulcan mind meld doesn't always work between the sexes. Beware of a woman who attempts to initiate eye contact because you know conversation cannot be far behind. She'll hover over you like a buzzard over a manure wagon! Do those disgusting things that will cause the woman who thinks she is *Mrs. Right* to turn and run away like a bat out of hell or at least ponder her next move.

For example:
➢ Pick your nose and eat what you pick (hence the term *picky-eater)*

- Pick up a butt off the floor and light up
- Drool—drool a lot—drool out of both sides of your mouth, drool out of your mind and into the spittoon you carry with you (personally monogrammed of course) Use exaggerated movements to determine if our armpits are still protected by today's deodorant use
- Turn sideways and give her a glimpse of that *before* protruding image of your abominable abdominal cavity
- Demonstrate your prowess as a manambalist (making fart sounds emanate from your hand) or similar sounds from underneath your armpits as you alternate pits in time with the music
- Provide a florid demonstration of the baseball player itch
- Pick your ear, remove your digit and sniff it as if to verify that the petrie dish sample came from your ear
- Scratch your head so much that she cannot decide whether you suffer from dandruff, the heartbreak of psoriasis, head lice or are simply in deep, confused thought
- Start talking to yourself and then answer yourself

In short, do your best to reach out…reach far out and disgust someone!

WARNING!

There are a small percentage of women who like

disgusting and tasteless men like you. Remember, *RB* (Rule Breakin') women will try to date any male that shows the slightest sign of life even if it is sustained by a respirator and interminable tubing. This warning, therefore, serves as due notice and your reading thereof exonerates the author if the above-specified strategies actually encourage rather than discourage the assumable *Mrs. Right.* Even the most disgusting of all men has his match in some dimension of the universe—of course, not necessarily our universe.

If you find that being disgusting and crude is actually encouraging the woman you are attempting to shy away from, tone down your uncouthness.

For example:
➤ Pick your nose and grin, but don't eat what you pick (hence the term *pickin' and grinin'*)
➤ Pick up a butt off the floor and put it in your pocket to enjoy in the privacy of your own home
➤ Drool out of only one side of your mouth and don't carry a spittoon
➤ Raise your hands slightly and sniff your armpits discreetly
➤ Never turn sideways—be forward by stepping backward
➤ Only play single armpit tunes
➤ Never itch yourself like you played any kind of sports
➤ Pick your ear, but realize what you're doing and nonchalantly hold that pose

> ➤ Scratch your head lightly to suggest dandruff only
> ➤ When you talk to yourself, never, never under any circumstances answer yourself.

So, beware of women who advance toward you or worse yet, ask you for a date. Remember, dating is like playing a game of *Old Maid*. No matter what great matches you make during the dating process, there is a high probability that in 20 years you will have a grumpy old woman on your hands. If you really want to know how your potential dating partner will fare with time, be sure to get in touch with her biological heritage and meet her mother; better yet, meet her grandmother or her great-grandmother. Count the rings—family trees don't lie! Especially be weary of *RB* women; indeed, they don't give a damn! They don't know how you feel. Nobody knows how a man really feels—except about beer and sports. Feelings, whoa, whoa, whoa, feelings...

Manifesto 2

Avoid Eye Contact with Women and for Heaven's Sake...Shut Up!

A big fuss is made of eye contact in psychiatry. The mature, emotionally balanced individual is able to initiate and sustain ocular contact. Presumably, those who inconsistently maintain, avert or avoid eye contact are less healthy, less assertive or attempting to hide something—or perhaps just legally blind.

Of course, there is always an exception to every rule. Those male individuals who gawk and ogle at women are blatantly transparent with an obvious modus operandi. If you are a male gawker or ogler, forget it! You are beyond hope. You stand there drooling and you are not only susceptible to the hook (or hooker), you likely invite such behavior with that wantoned look on your face. A quick wink or fleeting eye contact and you are putty in the hands of the winker. Dictate your last will and testament and have it notarized that you are legally insane for it is all over for you.

For the rest of us who don't see boobs in anything and everything that moves, try to reduce the psychological approach-avoidance conflict. There are many time-tested approaches you can use to avoid attempts by a *BR* woman to initiate the eye contact attack and its magnetic pull. Some of these avoidant strategies may be familiar to you.

For example:
- ➤ Think of the names of baseball players
- ➤ Calculate *pi* (22 divided by…Anyone? Anyone?)
- ➤ Become self-absorbed in the true meaning of life
- ➤ Think of something or some place real cold or freezing like the Arctic, ice cubes, winter in Minnesota or your ex-spouse
- ➤ Imagine yourself in cryogenic stasis
- ➤ Try to figure out with all the potential names for planets in our universe, why would anybody name 7th planet from the sun, 'Uranus'
- ➤ Review the sequence of steps required to stop your VCR clock from blinking 12:00
- ➤ Drool over surfing your television with a remote in one hand and a beer in the other
- ➤ Contemplate celibacy and a vocation to the priesthood
- ➤ Practice stand-up yoga and use your navel as a focal point
- ➤ Envision Mr. Potato Head or your favorite Chia-Pet
- ➤ Pretend it's April 15th of any year—procrastinators need no further explanation
- ➤ Think about your mother or the bearded lady
- ➤ Ponder, what is a Pee Wee Herman
- ➤ Two words: Transcendental Meditation
- ➤ Think about CPMS (see Manifesto 6)
- ➤ Think about another guy; well, maybe not. Do

whatever it takes to distract you from the gaze of *Mrs. Right.*

For those of you men who are not adept at such mind games, that is, you can best be characterized by the proverb—forgive me, if you are reading this book, you probably don't know what a proverb is...you can best be characterized by the saying, "Deep waters run very still," you must choose an alternative tactic to avoid the seductive eyes of vampy vamps. Remember:

Loose Eyes Sink Guys!

So, if you cannot magically manipulate the mental memories in the backseat of your mind, do one or more of the following:

➢ Avert your eyes and look elsewhere
➢ Cast your eyes downward and check to see if...

- ➤ Your shoes match
- ➤ You are wearing the same color socks
- ➤ You are wearing pants
- ➤ Your fly is up
- ➤ You have an inny or outty belly button—of course, this only works if you can actually see past your stomach!

However, if you are like the majority of men who can't gaze past your protruding abdominal cavity, try...

- ➤ Glance upwards and occupy your time by...

- ➤ Counting ceiling tiles
- ➤ Seeing if the corners of the room meet
- ➤ Looking for water spots
- ➤ Checking for asbestos or structural damage
- ➤ Identifying live or dead bugs
- ➤ Whistling a happy tune

Now, whether you are looking down or glancing up, periodically test the waters by stealing a glance ahead. Have your tactics worked? Did your dullness rub off on her? Has *Mrs. Right* lost interest in you? Is she gone? Is she still staring? Is she approaching? Is this Tuesday? Is their life after a near *Mrs.?*

If you've broken the seductive link—no problem. You've whimped out one more time. Perhaps for the last time, but one more time nonetheless. For the moment, you wear a smug look on your face. You think you are as invincible as Bond...James Bond! You not only narrowly escaped a dangerous situation, but your tux is unwrinkled and un*smirched.*

However, what if *Mrs. Right* persists? What if she is staring at you right now more intensely than before? What if she's no more than two inches off the port nostril of your proboscis? Well, hold onto your pheromones! Simple avoidance was ineffective. By your ineptness, you did not take the 'approach' out of the approach-avoidance conflict. The link was not broken. The vampress is headed your way and dusk is about to settle. A stake is not the answer. Now what do you do?

It is too late to worry about what you didn't do! Had you been successful at appearing distant, disgusting and aloof, you would not be reading this now. You'd be watching the playoffs and drinking beer! But you didn't, did you?

So isn't this just peachy! Now that *Mrs. Right* has made contact with you, the *RB* woman will want to talk your ear off until they bleed...but for Heaven's sake, Shut Up!

Shut up? Yes, shut up! Trust me on this. Don't try to be witting or wiggle your way out of this one. Begin using hand singles and pray that she who thinks she's *Mrs. Right* neither has a family history of deafness nor is knowledgeable in sign language. With any luck, she will think you are just a bit mental and leave you alone.

Of course, if she does know sign language, you are in big trouble because you do not have the slightest idea of what you are saying to her or what she is saying to you. You may conclude mistakenly that she is having a seizure. In this situation, it is best to discontinue making meaningless motions with your dyslexic digits as you might commit yourself to something that most certainly you will later regret...and please, if you don't know what you are doing, DO NOT apply CPR!

If she breeches your disguise and you find yourself in the dangerous situation of having to open your mouth, talk in prehistoric, monosyllabic, Neanderthal words. You certainly are not totally unaccustomed to such language.

For example:
➢ "yah"
➢ "ain't"
➢ "nah"
➢ "uh"
➢ "ugh"
➢ "grunt"

➤ "oink"
➤ "arg"
➤ "mmm"

If you don't think that you can remember such elegant verbiage, write down these words right now on your hands, stomach or whatever part of your body that is most visible to your naked eye. Nothing throws a woman off more than an intelligent, spud-appearing man with impeccable conversational skills!

Make up for what you're not saying in listening to what you're not hearing. This is not a matter of what you hear is what you get. If *Mrs. Right* is able to entrap you in a conversation, albeit one-sided, there is a hidden agenda behind each utterance. At least become the discriminating listener and do not take things at face value. A typical conversation might go like this:

WHAT SHE SAYS	WHAT HE HEARS
1. Hi.	1. I want something from you and no matter what you do, I'm going to get it from you.
2. What's your name?	2. I'll need your name for the legal documents when we go to court.
3. My, you have a nice house.	3. My stuff will fit quite well here.

4. How do you keep it so clean?

4. Don't expect me to start cleaning house, doing laundry, washing windows, etc.

5. Been here long?

5. How fast will it take you to move out?

6. Are you financially independent?

6. I won't lower my standards and even if you have to work two or three jobs, you will keep me living at the level to which I am accustomed.

7. What do you do for entertainment?

7. We will go to the dinner theater and symphony—the remote control will be burned.

8. Yes, sex is important in a marriage *infrequently.*

8. You ask yourself, "Is and I believe in it that one or two words?"

9. Well, it's getting late and I'd better go.

9. What a bore, get me out of here and don't spare the pleasantries.

10. Bye.

10. What a pathetic excuse for a man; I don't even care if he has a pulse!

Manifesto C

Go Somewhere Else When She Tells You Where To Go

If you failed at Manifestos 1 and 2, you still have time to manipulate and control the situation. Women have told men where to go since prehistoric times. Like the old joke, they say that *God* created Adam before Eve so he would have at least one chance to say something! And the Adams have been losing ground ever since.

Before the term "dog house" entered our vernacular, "dino cave" was the banishment of a by-gone era. Testosterone Rex was in vogue and the foreshadowing of things to come were put into place. Men would have no direction at all in their lives if women did not tell them when to go, where to go, and how to go about going!

Well that is the illusion: let women think that you have no destiny of your own, that you have no direction in your life—even if the assertion is probably true. Control is just a state of mind and if you don't mind, it doesn't matter. Allow *Mrs. Right* to suggest where to go, but counter with a seemingly sensible and benign reason why it would make sense to go somewhere else, somewhere of your choosing. At all cost, maintain the appearance or at least the illusion that you are in control!

Illusion is defined as an erroneous perception of reality or a misconception. This is the crux of the matter. Control by man has always been a misconception as man has never been able to conceive —well, perhaps that is an incorrect analogy. Or is it simply another illusion?

Illusion or not, you are not going to pay a lot for this evening. Perhaps nothing. After all, you don't know this woman although you are sure she is a loser.

Why would she be attempting to make contact with you if she wasn't? Just like the old *Woody Allen* joke about you wouldn't want to be a member of any club that was willing to take you as a member.

Mrs. Right may be thinking of fine cuisine, but you are at best thinking of fast chow. After all, there is no real difference between a burger and prime rib. You know, the kind of place where she won't be able to change her order (as a woman has the right). You already left the clown in the box and are approaching the drive-up window—way too late to head back in reverse. Remember, you are in control even if you only think you are in control. Be a man even if your name is Whimpy!

A good rule of thumb is…if you have not been there, you are not going to start going there now. Chances are that if you haven't been there, you can't afford it anyway or you don't have the fashion sense to step foot in such a classy place. *Mrs. Right* will want you to pay through the nose early on in the relationship so that you will be accustomed to perpetual nosebleeds throughout the expanse of your association.

But that is not going to happen. Women made the mistake awhile back of wanting equal rights. Women can do anything that men can do—and sometimes they can do it better. They can open doors. They can mow the lawn. They can change the oil on the family truckster. They can remotely surf the family TV. They can hold a job. They can take out the garbage. They can use two cans of *Raid* to kill a bug the size of a fingernail just as well as men can. You are a *RB* woman! Let's hear you squeak!

So, where does *Mrs. Right* want to go? You may not know what she has in mind, but you do know where you don't want to go. After all, *Mrs. Right* has a job. If you go someplace other than "something" in the box where you can only hear every other word due to low volume and high crackle, let her pay. After all, a guest is a guest. She invited you. Guests don't pay. And the days—or knights—of chivalry are dead. You don't have to volunteer to do anything. You maintained the essence of control…for now.

Manifesto 4

Hep 10...27...51...Hike!

If you do not know where to go, TIME OUT! Take a HIKE! Literally. It is time for you to step back and mull things over. Do not think of it as *running* away. Think of it has a strategic move in order to plan your next strategic move even if the move forward is a step backward. There is nothing shameless in a strategic retreat! Like an artist, it sometimes helpful to stand back from the canvas or in your case, the *RB* woman. So go hiking, enjoy the solitude, wind in your face and allergies up your nose. Plan your next scheme, but make it a good one!

For those couch potatoes who need some stimulation in order to move more than one body part at a time, the following song parodies of hiking will serve to set the proper ambiance. Your goal if you choose to accept is to think of strategies to counteract the diabolical schemes of the *RB* woman. In case you fail, *man*kind will disavow any knowledge of your pitiful existence. Good luck, Jim!

Edward Galluzzi

THE BALLAD OF HIKER MAN
(SUNG TO THE BALLAD OF GILLIGAN'S ISLAND)

Just sit right back and you'll hear a tale.
A tale of a Hiker Man!
He started hiking long ago,
Before hiking was grand.

Yes, he is a mighty Hiker Man
Who leads us down dirt paths.
If he retired anytime soon,
Oh, woe, what would we do?
Oh, what would we do?

Well, things would sure start getting rough;
If Hiker Man was not our boss.
We'd take many paths over hill and dale
And soon we'd all be lost.
Soon we'd all be lost.

So each and every one of us,
Should mark each path we take.
If Hiker Man fades in a cloud of dust,
Rangers may find our fate.
Yes, they may find our fate!

WALTZ OF EAGLE CREEK PARK
(SUNG TO THE TENNESSEE WALTZ)

I was hiking, avoiding Mrs. Right, through Eagle Creek
Park;
When a small doe nearby I did spot.
I said, "so sorry," to my loved one and left her standing
there;
A buck stole her away from me!

I remember the hike and the Eagle Creek Waltz,
Now I know what that stray doe did cost!
Yes, I lost Mrs. Right the night they were playing,
The beautiful Eagle Creek Waltz.

Mrs. Right, she did left me, since I strayed from the
main path,
What price does a doe and buck cost?
I was thankful, very thankful and even happy
That I lost Mrs. Right to a buck!
[Chorus]
Well, I avoided, Mrs. Right for one more time,
With no doe not even a buck.
I was walking and back hiking to the great Eagle Creek
Waltz,
When another Mrs. Right I did spot!
[Chorus]

SORE FEET, SORE FEET
(SUNG TO THE TUNE "NEW YORK, NEW YORK")

Start spreadin' the news,
We're hiking today.
I wanna be no part of it
Sore Feet, Sore Feet!

These hiking boot blues
Are lingering today.
Trying to avoid Mrs. Right.
Sore Feet, Sore Feet!

I wanna wake up Saturday morn and go
back to sleep.
To find my…
Head on the floor,
Bod in a heap,
Feet that are sore,
Still need some sleep!

These hiking boot blues
Are melting away.
I'll make a brand new start of it,
Sore Feet, Sore Feet!

If I can avoid her now,
Surely I can avoid her then.
When I hike again
No More, No More!

UNDER THE TREES
(SUNG TO "OVER THE RAINBOW")

Somewhere, under the tall trees
Flowers bloom wild.
Hikers walk amuck the paths,
Catch that ivy, hope it's mild!

Somewhere, over muddy paths,
Forest stuff stays.
Until it globs on your shoes,
Then you take it away!

Someday we'll wish upon a star,
And deer will come close rather than stay afar.
We'll stop and smell the roses, wow,
Bees bite noses, first aid kits we need right now.

Somewhere, in the parking lot,
Hikers rest.
Now it is time to go back
To the single's world fest!

HIKERS WILL COME OUT TOMORROW
(SUNG TO "TOMORROW" FROM ANNIE)

Hikers will come out tomorrow
Bet your bottom penny that tomorrow,
There'll be some.

Just thinking about that hiking
Our eyes glisten with tears and sorrow,
Allergies, anyone?

When we're stuck on a path that's wet and muddy;
We just stick out our tongues, and sneer, and say:

Oh, I'll stay in bed on Saturday.
Hiking will just wait until tomorrow,
Come what may.

Tomorrow, tomorrow, I'll see ya, tomorrow,
Please let me sleep today!
Tomorrow, tomorrow, I'll see ya, tomorrow,
Just stay away today!

YOU HIKE UP OUR LIVES
(SUNG TO "YOU LIGHT UP MY LIFE")

So many paths,
We've hiked near' all of them.
Up and down hills
And beyond yon dales.

Singles in file,
Changing their positions.
Chat for awhile,
And change once again.

Mrs. Right, enters my space.
Gives me no hope, to carry on.
So I stay straight on the path
So I don't have—to scratch!

As the hike ends,
Hunger takes hold of us.
Our body mends,
At Men's Bar-R-Us!

So many dreams,
We keep deep inside us.
Hiking again,
Avoiding Mrs. Right-us.
[Chorus]

THIS DAY WAS MADE FOR HIKING
(SUNG TO "THIS LAND IS YOUR LAND")

If it's freezing out,
If it's steaming out,
If it's real rainy out,
If it's real windy out,
If it's muddy out,
If it's hazy out,
Then this day was made for hiking!

So if you're hiking
And the sun is out.
You're probably dreaming
There really is no doubt!

So go back to bed,
It's all in your head.
Then this day was made for sleeping!

HIKIN' IN THE RAIN
(SUNG TO "SINGIN" IN THE RAIN")

Hikin' in the rain,
Just hikin' in the rain.
What a glorious feeling
I'm hikin' again.
I'm gazing at deer
So stoned face with fear.
Looking up for dove
Never ready for love.

So, come on with the rain.
I've a smirk on my face;
I'll walk with no pain
At a very slow pace.
And singin' in the rain.

HIKE
(SUNG TO "HAIR")

They ask me why,
I'm just a hikin' guy.
I'm hikin' noon and night,
Ain't that a fright!

I'm hiking high and low,
Don't ask me why, don't know.
It's not for need of exercise,
Or what to do otherwise.

Singles, want to take a long hike,
Long beautiful hike.
Shining, freezing, steaming, flaxen, waxen.

Hikin' down the path, yah!
Trippin' over roots, yah!
Here hiker, there hiker
Everywhere hiker, hiker.
Hike, hike, hike, hike, hike, hike, hike.

HIKING IS THE NAME
(SUNG TO THE THEME FROM CHEERS:
"WHERE EVERYBODY KNOWS YOUR NAME")

Making your way in the world today
Mrs. Right wants ev'rything you've got.
Taking a break from all your worries
Sure would help a lot.
Wouldn't you like to get away?

Sometimes you wanna go where nobody
knows your name,
And they don't care that you came.
You wanna be where Mrs. Right can't
call you by name,
You wanna hike where nobody knows
your name.

Hiking Saturdays is what we do
Believe it or do not.
Gives us a chance to argue and shout.
Sure does help a lot.
Wouldn't you like to get away?
[Chorus]

Well, I certainly hope that was inspirational to you and provided you the opportunity to ponder your next move on how to avoid the clutches of Mrs. Right. If you came up dry and have no idea of your next move, read on to help reduce the odds of first contact.

Manifesto E

Divest Yourself of All Communicative Devices and Reduce the Odds of First Contact

Learn to isolate and cloak yourself in today's world. Take a lesson from the Catholic nuns of old who not only took a vowel of poverty, but also a vowel of silence. They neither talked to each other or to the outside world. A hollow, cylindrical wooden tube was used like a turnstile to pass objects back and forth with no contact or communication with the sender. Isolate yourself and reduce the odds of "first contact."

If I might diverse a little, I have had personal experience with women who have taken the vowel of silence. Oh, what a wonderful world this would be... Actually, I was an altar boy attending a Good Friday Catholic service at a local convent. For you pagans, a convent is not a criminal blowing off steam! It is a cloister of nuns and the good sisters at this particular convent took the vowel of silence. The nuns did not interact with the outside world. There was no Internet for them. They were never on-line. As mentioned earlier, this particular convent used this rotating, wooden tube to transfer material. A pull of a rope rang a bell signaling that the material was ready for transfer.

This was a pretty efficient system unless the hearing impaired nun was on duty that day!

A friend of mine was with me and we began arguing whether or not he could fit inside the tube. After much serious debate between the two of us, he decided on the direct approach and jumped in the tube. As my friend crouched in the tube, I impulsively pulled the rope. It seem liked the natural thing to do. Carpe Diem! The bell rang and the cylinder began rotating.

My friend, who was about to pick up some good habits, disappeared into the swallowing jowls of the convent.

My friend was gone in an instant. I imagined, like in a *Star Trek* episode where the transporters went amuck, he would return in this melted, molten mess of mucous membranes! I began firing off prayers like it was my last anointing and Satan was hot on my tail.

After several long minutes, the tube rotated back slowly. My friend gradually appeared, seemingly whole, with an embarrassed reddened face that would put a sunset to shame. I asked my friend what had happened and what did he see. However, he was in a trance-like state and unable to mutter a single sound. My friend, to this day, has taken the vowel of silence. Well, sorry about the personal diversion...

Men who are being pursued by *RB* women should consider these cloaking options:

➢ While everybody is getting online, get offline!
➢ Avoid the Internet—assume the World Wide Web is

a busy international spider spinning its web and you have arachnophobia

➢ Don't answer your e-mail; better yet, turn your e-mail address into a dead letter box—that is, d-mail!

➢ Sell your car, cycle, bike, tricycle or transporter— you're not going anywhere

➢ Quit your job to further your anonymity—cloaking does not require any expenditures

➢ Do not carry beepers or cellular phones

➢ Unplug your answering machine at home and while you are at it, take out your phone—you really don't need to communicate with the outside world because you know they *will find* you if they really need you

➢ Do not use credit cards or other traceable forms of transactions

➢ Do not accept telegrams or flowers bearing Trojan secrets

➢ Stop your mail and never use your home address— get a post office box if you absolutely have to *receive* junk mail or even less important mail

And, if all these strategies fail and women are still able to locate you, place an obituary in the local newspaper! Extinguish your distinguished existence on earth by exploring and employing every avenue available.

If you follow these simple cloaking maneuvers, you will no longer be a blemish on the ozone of the earth. However, if for some inexplicable reason *Mrs. Right* links up with you anyway, do not for any reason download any information.

WARNING! VIRUSES!

Now a virus has been defined as a worm with a Trojan horse or bomb attached to it. Sound familiar ladies? A worm is simply a program that replicates itself...kind of like masturbation taken to excess! Like Greek mythology, a Trojan horse is something that represents itself as something it is not. Sound familiar men?

Specifically, here, we are talking about the dreaded *Wedded Virus.* It is a ring virus that attaches itself to you, by vowel, for life and begins changing your structure almost immediately. It promises for better although it makes you worse. If it doesn't work out, it takes your riches and leaves you poorer. And even until death do your part is no certainty of separation. You must inoculate yourself before you become infected. It's the only way to avoid any virus, including the *human*kind.

If you cannot isolate yourself by cloaking, try cloning—sort of like "if you can't beat them, join them!" If *RB* women must communicate with you, wear them down! Send multiples of yourself among the multitudes. Why not two? Why not three? If scientists can clone sheep and monkeys, cloning the male member of mankind should not be a far stretch for the DNA. After all, men have been called "apes" and "sheep" among other things throughout human history. The *RB* woman won't know what hit her. She will be confused by her inability to wear you down and eventually terminate her attempts at communicating with you.

Manifesto 6

Avoid Women with CPMS

Well, if you can't avoid the clutches of *Mrs. Right,* at least be aware of the PMS/CPMS distinction. Women generally have PMS (Pre-Menstrual Syndrome), but most women progress to CPMS (Chronic Pre-Menstrual Syndrome). Now, the difference between PMS and CPMS is as forceful as the difference between casually dating a woman and living/being married to one. In the former, you get periodic respites from the relationship and in the latter there is no escape—much like conjoint twins you are bound together with no hope for surgery except a painful separation or divorce!

Although you cannot necessarily avoid dating a woman who has PMS, the *sensitive* male can learn to discern the difference between PMS and CPMS women:

PMS WOMEN

1. Changes her mind quickly
2. Is irritable at times

CPMS WOMEN

1. Never changes her mind, is always right
2. Find her picture in the dictionary next to the word "irritable"

3. Says she "hates" you on the first date

3. Says she "hates" you now more than ever on the second date

4. Becomes whiny and clingy

4. Doesn't say a word, just stares at you

5. Tells you that her life is hell

5. Suffers from demonic possession

6. Throws objects at you

6. Throws you against objects

7. Asks you to "forgive" her even though she did nothing wrong

7. Demands an apology from you even though you did nothing wrong

8. Cries at the movies when everybody else is laughing

8. Cries at the same moment watching the movie five years later

9. Tells you where to go

9. Tells you where to go, how to get there and what will happen if you come back

10. Is demanding and Controlling

10. Orders you to rewrite your will

PMS is the gift of women and the curse of men. CPMS is the nail in the coffin of *man*kind. It is the license for women to justify their actions even legally in a court of law. No man is safe. What was once prosecuted as a homicide becomes justifiable menstruation. A messy brief indeed, but nonetheless a defensible one.

Learn not to patronize women with PMS or CPMS. It is one thing for them to attribute their actions to either condition, but if you value your life, don't you ever query, "Is it that time of the month?" Amusing perhaps years ago, but now certainly grounds for harassment. And so what if it is that "time of the month?" What can you do about it other than batten down the hatches and hold on for the ride?

I hope you are not the sentimental, sympathetic-type kind of guy. If you are, you will surely fall for SHAM PMS or CPMS. SHAM PMS or CPMS is used by a woman who attributes her negative, hostile or unpredictable actions to the condition when it's not only "that time of month," but "that time of month" was over with two days ago or two weeks ago! Don't be enticed by the SHAM because it will certainly cost you something; perhaps cost you more than you can afford!

Manifesto G

Remember, You're Not Just a Piece of Meat

Sure, the *sensitive* male is taught to...

- ➢ open doors
- ➢ carry luggage
- ➢ kill bugs
- ➢ wait endlessly during shopping sprees
- ➢ send flowers
- ➢ relinquish the TV remote control
- ➢ run errands
- ➢ lift heavy stuff
- ➢ lift not so heavy stuff
- ➢ take out the garbage
- ➢ open windows in the middle of the night
- ➢ mow the lawn
- ➢ put a worm on the pole
- ➢ gut fish and cut off their heads
- ➢ debug the computer
- ➢ close windows in the middle of the night
- ➢ fix the car
- ➢ clean the gutters
- ➢ edge the lawn
- ➢ trim the bushes

➢ clean up dog chips
➢ unclog the drains
➢ fertilize the yard
➢ grill meat (arg! arg! arg!)
➢ unclog the toilet
➢ put the toilet seat down
➢ …and anything else she can think of

These certainly are not innate abilities and must be taught much like teaching a kitten to purge itself in the litter box. What the *sensitive* male is taught seems as endless and bottomless as a black hole. But men, you're not just a piece of meat on a hook! You're not just an animal! You're a human bean!

The woman who considers herself to be your *Mrs. Right* will want to lure you into her web and exploit you even though you may not be "that kind of man!" You're not just a breeder! Remember, you are more than just an object. Not much more albeit to the *RB* woman, but a teeny, weenie bit more. Of course, once women figure out how they themselves can compensate for that "teeny, weenie bit more" man will become just objects. An appendage to be tossed out when it is no longer needed or becomes troublesome and bothersome (e.g., an appendix). Man will become an object that gathers common dust and will only be dusted at the whim of the *RB* woman—like a bust of Shakespeare given as a bargain gift from a cheap friend.

The *sensitive* male has to un-teach himself to counteract the exploitation of *RB* women. I know this is difficult guys, but you have to let women:

➤ Open doors (remember, chivalry is dead!)
➤ Let women carry their own luggage, as you will have that one, small brief case to carry that has enough clothes to last two weeks plus toiletries
➤ Let bugs roam freely and take over the house if they want to (besides, bugs will probably keep it cleaner than you could ever do)
➤ Shop for things that you want and don't wait endlessly during her shopping spree (that's right, go to the Men's Store at *Sears and* get those power tools!)
➤ Don't ever send flowers—don't even take fake flowers from the cemetery or pull them out of your neighbors flower bed
➤ Of all that is holy, never ever give up control over the TV remote control—men, this is yours by divine right, so do not bring shame upon yourself and all of *man*kind
➤ The only running you will be doing is jogging, running errands are simply out of the question—you have more valuable things to do with your time, like guzzling beer, passing gas, etc.
➤ Lifting heavy stuff may injure your back or give you a hernia men, so let women do it—they're likely to suffer from Osteoporosis, Scoliosis (lateral S-curve in the back) or Kyphosis (curve that hunches back) anyway—no sense in disfiguring yourself
➤ Taking out the garbage is a historical rite that is deep

in tradition and steep in ritual—this is man's sacred ground and almost genetic in nature—man should continue taking out the garbage, even for *RB* women, it's the very least we can do

➤ Open and closing windows at night do not fall in man's purview—for one, men typically sleep through the evening with no worries or babies to nurse and two, men typically run fans at night for comfort and for white noise to block out nightly distractions (like women asking for the window to be opened or closed)—so men, don't fool with windows

➤ Mowing the lawn, cleaning gutters, trimming bushes, etc. have traditionally been identified with men to provide him respite and solace from the demands of family life or wife—however, women more and more are taking up such yardly duties which is of great consequence to men—we do not want to lose are meditation, rehab and recovery time for it costs us nothing and gives us everything, so chain the lawn mower, hide the gas can, take off the cutting blade or conceal the spark plug-whatever it takes to maintain that domain handed down to you from your father, grandfather, great grandfather, great-great grandfather and the cave men of old

➤ Putting worms on fishing poles and gutting fish is not so bad—go ahead and permit women to request such activities from you, but be sure to leave the cooking up to them

➤ Debugging the computer is not the same as taking a

broom to your computer or spraying your computer with *Raid*—however, this is another isolated activity for men to continue as women, especially *RB* women, will generally avoid at all cost giving man peace and tranquility online—not to mention other things—women's knowledge tends to be limited in this area and can be demonstrated by asking her a simple question: What is the difference between a parallel and serial port? If she's a *RB* woman, she'll reply that the one that gets soggy when you pour milk on it is the serial port!

➢ Finally, don't put the toilet sit down—don't give away one of the few exercises that women perform with their upper bodies—it is like exercising their mind and *RB* women secretly enjoy the activity even though they outwardly complain loudly about it.

Manifesto H

A Dog is a Man's Best Friend

It is only a myth that you must have a date and it is even a greater myth that if you have a date it has to be on Saturday night. The Saturday night dating myth is based actually in how the days of the week were initially identified. Of course, you do remember what the seven days of the week are, don't you? No, not five; there are seven days counting the weekend: Sunday, Monday, Tuesday, Wednesday, Thursday, Friday and Saturday.

What you may not know or remember is the origin of naming the days of the week. They are based on gods of ancient mythology. Please, stay with me on this one and you eventually know why people have the myth that you must have a date on Saturday night. Once you understand the myth, you can be free of its influences on your life.

SUNDAY

Sunday, not to be confused with William Ashly Sunday (1862-1935) the evangelist (although his last name does seem more than just coincidental), is commonly known as the first day of the week. It is the day of the Sol, the "best" or "most" as in Sunday clothes or Sunday punch. You can't date on a Sunday because the dates you are able to secure are not the "best" or "most." Nobody dates on a Sunday for this reason.

MONDAY

The second day of the week, Monday, is the day of the moon. You will find that most people commit crimes or are committed to a mental health facility on Monday. This is definitely not a good day to date unless incarceration of one type or another appeals to you.

TUESDAY

Tuesday, the third day of the week, is the day of the war god. Nobody dates on Tuesdays because the concept of war goes against everything that dating stands for. Or does it?

WEDNESDAY

The fourth day of the week, Wednesday, is otherwise known as Woden's Day. I know this sounds like something the three Stooges would say; however, Woden is the chief god of the pagan Anglo-Saxons. Now, pagan Anglo-Saxon probably describes each and every one of you in some way or the other! However, celebrating pagans is hardly a way to start a relationship and dating is better left for another day.

THURSDAY

Thursday, the fifth day of the week, honors Thor, the Norse god of thunder and the sky who is armed with a magical hammer. Now, I don't know about you, but I don't think I want those kinds of surprises on a date. I mean a magical hammer. What can you do with a magical hammer on a date? Huh?

FRIDAY

The sixth day of the week is Friday in celebration of Freya, the Norse god of peace and fertility. Now, at first glance, Friday would seem to be the best day of the week for the mythical date. Ah, peace. Doesn't that sound peaceful? Ah, fertility. Whoops! Fertility does not seem to be a good thing for a date. Perhaps two's company and three's a crowd best fits here. This is where you get married first and then date afterwards.

SATURDAY

Ah, Saturday. Saturday is the seventh day of the week and so named in honor of Saturn, the Roman god of agriculture. Kind of like you reap what you sow. Saturday, however, is more commonly known for the "Saturday night special," a cheap, small caliber handgun that is easily attainable and concealable. Now, if that does not describe a *RB* woman and her actions, I don't know what does! Hence, the myth that you not only must have a date, but that it must happen on Saturday night.

Dating is simply a state of mind and if you don't mind, it doesn't matter. If you need warmth and intimacy, a dog or cat will give you the same thing as a woman...except that there is no cost and hardly any payback for an act of kindness as well, except maybe a bone, treat or something. Moreover, you can pet a pet and not be accused of sexual harassment unless you go in for that sort of thing. If you have fallen for the myth of not being alone on Saturday night, then you weaklings can lease a pet once a week on Saturday. Go to Pets-R-Us. Or better yet, visit your local humane society and find a companion for a lifetime.

Manifesto I

Stupid Excuses to Get Out of a Date Even if *Mrs. Right* is at Your Door

If you are a weak male and have been unable to follow Manifestos 1, 2, *C,* 4, E, 6, G and H, there is still hope for you, albeit little to no hope. Remember two rules: always look out for number one and don't step in number two! If the word "no" on your lips was replaced by the word "maybe" or "yes," heaven help you and pay real good attention to this Manifesto. It may be your last hope, you pathetic representation of the male homosapien!

For the stronger male who has not already agreed to the date from hell, the following excuses can be used to avoid a date. These 50 ways to leave a date can be used singularly or mixed together depending on the push of the female persuasion. To avoid a date at all cost and the most pushiness of all *RB* women, use all of them!

Tried and *tested* excuses that can be used to avoid a date:

1. You sound like a very nice woman and I would love to go out with you, but I have this very contagious disease...

2. My evangelist has informed me that Wednesday of next week will be the end of the world...
3. I'm sorry, I'm Jewish and we cannot do anything on Saturday night that is similar to work...
4. I stopped dating once them sexual harassing things were passed...
5. I gave up *RB* women for Lent...
6. Hello, my name is Ben and I'm gay...
7. I live with my parents and they would lose me as a deduction if I begin dating...
8. I'm sorry; I'm on a *fat*-free diet...
9. It's against my religion...
10. I'm really a nun in priest's clothing...
11. I'm sorry; I'm awful busy trying to keep my VCR from flashing 12:00...
12. Are you kidding? Look what Eve did to Adam...
13. I'm chronically single and was told it's terminal...
14. I'm sorry, I'm from the J.W. Bobbit family and we're not permitted to get involved with women anymore...
15. I just got a gift certificate for a vasectomy...
16. I just had a sex change operation and I'm not that kind of girl...
17. Never on a Sunday, a Monday, a Tuesday...
18. Sorry, I give at the office...
19. My professional psychic told me that I would

not meet my true love until the year 2025...

20. My parents never told me about the "birds and the bees..."
21. By law, I'm required to tell you that I get my dating tips from the *Bob and Tom Show*...
22. They only let me out on holidays...
23. I only have one strike left with the new three strikes and your out law...
24. Being Italian, my godfather must approve of you...
25. My doctor warned me that on this type of medication, I should only go out with women during my drug-free holidays...

Tired and *untested* excuses that can be used to get out of a date, even if a *RB* woman is on your doorsteps:

1. I'm sorry I won't be able to keep our date and I tried to call you before you left, but my mother, father, uncle, great aunt, third cousin and best friend died about an hour ago and...
2. My clothes are being *martinized* and I have to pick them up in about an hour...
3. Say while running out the front door: "I accidentally swallowed my canary and am heading for the hospital's emergency room..."
4. My church informed me that tonight will be the end of the world and I promised my mother that I would spend it with her...

5. My doctor just called; he gave me 24 hours to live and I don't want to spend my last night with a *RB* woman...

6. Darn it, I forgot you were coming and I'm in the middle of watching Vanna on *Wheel of Fortune*...

7. I forgot my ex-wife is being executed at the state prison this evening...

8. Say while running out the front door: "Sorry, I just spotted Elvis and Colonel Parker" (for my cousin, Toni)...

9. A UFO just landed in my backyard and they want me to take a little ride with them...

10. Oh, I can't now 'cause the cable company finally called and said they will be right over...

11. I am Amish; I can't drive or ride in a car and my horse just died...

12. I can't get over how much you look like my mother...

13. Quickly reverse the numbers of your address on your home and mailbox...

14. Let her know that you are a Jehovah's Witness, Amway salesman and are looking into Avon...

15. Insult her looks or if she is real ugly, be honest about how you feel about her...

16. Tell her that you forgot that it is your turn to stand guard over the cinnamon bun with the likeness of Mother Teresa...

17. Quickly put yellow crime scene tape across your door and windows...
18. Are you kidding; the *Rosie O'Donnell Show* is just starting...
19. Look, there goes the *Energizer* bunny...
20. Ask a police friend to come by in his cruiser and scream over a megaphone: "Come out with your hands up; we have your place surrounded!"...
21. Tell her that you have an evil twin and it was he who arranged the date...
22. Tell her that you cannot leave your computer right now because it has a virus and high fever...
23. Start talking about life insurance and tell her operators are standing by...
24. Sit on the porch waiting while you carve your tombstone...
25. Dial 1-800-DATE-BE-GONE...

Manifesto 10

Make Your First Date Your Last Date and Make It Last Only 5 Minutes

You pathetic, useless, meaningless, spineless... You're going out on a date, aren't you? You're reading this Manifesto because you didn't have the guts to follow the preceding Manifestos and you're going out on a date. Well that's just fine! I don't even know why I talk to you anymore except that there is, believe or not, still a slim hope that you can get out of the mess in which you find yourself. And I bet you spend most of your life having others clean up the messes you make you worthless weenie worm of a man. I almost should end this Manifesto now and let you lay in the mess you created for yourself. Be thankful I am sensitive, kindhearted and still willing to share with you how to regain your single status of singledom (or singledumb).

It is important that you put the kibosh on expanded information, which a *RB* woman gives you as she attempts to spill her guts in the first minute of your contact (ugh, date). Remember; tell your date that if you wanted her social history, you would have been a psychologist. It is important, real important, that you nip this attempt at significant and intimate interchange in the bud. The objective of this Manifesto is to point out to you the typical warning signs in a woman's letting of her social history that are attempts at gaining sympathy (males aren't capable of empathy) and exploit the male character—or is that caricature?

Like the gut spilling of all social histories, the *RB* woman is likely to start at the beginning: birth. She will tell you that she was born out of diversity to gain immediate sympathy, that is, premature birth, club nose, two umbilical cords, web hair, a tail...it does not matter. The *RB* woman will tell you that she was challenged from birth or before birth if that's possible.

If the sensitive male remains unsympathetic, the *RB* woman will then detail her challenges through her developmental years. She will tell you that she never crawled and did not walk until she was three. She never uttered single words like "mamma" and "dadda," but spoke in sentences like "I like expensive gifts and to be taken expensive places." The *RB* woman gazes at you longingly to determine if you got her drift. She will tell you that she has never achieved bladder or bowel control and remark, "Some of my men like that."

If you let her, the *RB* woman will continue spilling her history. She will detail hospitalizations and surgeries in attempts to rid herself of the heartbreak of psoriasis. She will tell you about the anguish pain she suffered during plastic surgery to change her belly button from an outty to an inny. If that does not make you swell with tears, she'll tell you how she had to endure electrolysis to rid herself of that bothersome moustache. She will look at you wearily and tell you how she had to attend public schools.

Now, the *RB* woman can see in your eyes that your defenses are waning. She increases the stakes and heads for the jugular as you find out that her parents were killed when she was ten, how she lost her way in life in despair and took up tobacco, alcohol and other drug use such as milk. The *RB* woman gazes at you knowingly and realizes she's got you in the palm of her hands. She continues by telling you about her rehab and recovery at the Levy Shevy clinic in Detroit. She tells you how she entered the clinic three times before she was finally able to give up the milk.

The *RB* woman will tell you that she has found peace, tranquility and stability. She will have you convinced that she is a better person now. She has not only faced insurmountable adversities in her life, but that she has met each challenge with undeniable success. The *RB* woman's tale has you reaching for your charge card in your back pocket and you are ready to purchase that diamond wedding ring. You hardly know this woman, but find that you must marry her—dating can come later. The trap has been set and the door is closed shut. You are in deep, deep troubbbbbbbbbbbb—le!

Heh! Don't fall for this. Everybody faces tragedy in his or her life one-way or the other. Try to remember that you were not born yesterday; so try not to act like it! Realize that not only has the *RB* woman monopolized the date, but also that she's gone way beyond five minutes.

You need to recognize the social history dialog of

RB women and learn how to intervene with it. It's time to play "one upmanship." Nothing turns off a *RB* woman more than a man who presents a worse social history than she fabricated.

So, if the *RB* woman tells you she was born two months premature, tell her that you were born three months premature. Add that you had no umbilical cord and spent the six months of pregnancy bouncing around in your mother's womb suffering bruises and contusions. Counter that you don't remember your developmental years because aliens abducted you and they erased your memory. Tell her how your parents never worked and you held two jobs by the age of twelve to support their habits. Tell her you didn't have time to attend public schools or any school—that you learned on the streets. Tell her…, well, you may have not noticed, but your *RB* date left five minutes ago. You got carried away about your pitiful life. You did well and should definitely consider enrolling in acting school. You avoided your date with dentistry!

Manifesto 11

Sell Your House and Blend Invisibly With the Homeless

You! Yes, you! You just don't get it do you? You're pathetic. Not only did you accept a date, but also you actually let the first date go beyond 5 minutes, didn't you? Well, it's not like I didn't warn you. You stupid son of a bitch! I laid out Manifestos 1, 2, *C*, 4, E, 6, G, H, I and 10. You either are too Neanderthal to follow these Manifestos or you are illiterate. But here you are at Manifesto 11 and now you're begging me for ways of providing you anonymity. As usual, your testosterone level was higher than your IQ. You whiner! You got yourself involved with a woman *via* the first date and now you feel that your space is invaded. Well, isn't that just peachy?

MANIFESTO 1

Manifesto 1 was your chance to nip it right in the bud before anything got started. You were suppose to shy away from women who showed the slightest interest in you by doing those disgusting things that cause women to turn around and run away like bats out of hell! You did not follow *Manifesto 1,* did you?

MANIFESTO 2

Manifesto 2 warned you about making eye contact with women, particularly *RB* women. The saying, *Loose eyes sink guys,* was offered to you as a reminder. If you were unsuccessful and eye contact progressed to chit-chat, you were instructed to "shut up!" You did not follow *Manifesto 2,* did you?

MANIFESTO C

Manifesto C suggested that you go somewhere else when the assumable *Mrs. Right* tells you where to go. She may be thinking of fine cuisine when at best you are thinking of fast chow. You were suppose to follow the rule of thumb: If you have not been there, you are not going to start going there now. You did not follow *Manifesto C,* did you?

MANIFESTO 4

Manifesto 4 instructed you to take a hike, literally. It was your opportunity to step back and review your situation with a critical eye. A number of parody songs were added about hiking for those couch potatoes who cannot move more than one muscle at a time. You did not follow *Manifesto 4,* did you?

MANIFESTO E

Manifesto E tried to teach you to isolate and cloak yourself. You were to devoid yourself of all communicative devices in order to reduce the odds of first contact. While everybody was getting on-line, you were supposed to get off-line to avoid downloading the dreaded *Wedded Virus.* You did not follow *Manifesto E,* did you?

MANIFESTO 6
Manifesto 6 attempted to make you aware of the distinction between *PMS* and *CPMS* women in the event that you actually were foolish enough to get caught up in dating. *CPMS* gives women the license to justify their actions civilly as well as in a court of law. It warned you that no man is safe. You did not follow *Manifesto 6,* did you?

MANIFESTO G
Manifesto G reminded you that you are not just a piece of meat! You're more than just an object! What the sensitive male is taught by *RB* women is as bottomless as a black hole. You are taught how not to be exploited by *Mrs. Right.* Remember, chivalry is dead! You did not follow *Manifesto G,* did you?

MANIFESTO H
Manifesto H diffused the myth that not only must you have a date, but also it has to be on Saturday night. The origins of the days of the week were traced from their link with the gods of ancient mythology. You learned how a *RB* woman is like a "Saturday night special." You were taught pet substitutions. You did not follow *Manifesto H,* did you?

MANIFESTO I

Manifesto I artfully identified for your those stupid excuses you can use to get out of a date even if *Mrs. Right* was on your doorstep (e.g., "I forgot, my ex-wife is being executed at the State prison this evening"). You were presented 50 all time great excuses to fend off at the last minute that would be date. You did not follow *Manifesto I,* did you?

MANIFESTO 10

Manifesto 10 attempted to get you out of an unfortunate situation. It described how to make your first date your last date and make it last only five minutes. You learned how *Mrs. Right* used her social history to her advantage and how you could fabricate a better history in playing the game, "One-Upmanship." You did not follow *Manifesto 10,* did you?

MANIFESTO 11

So, your pitiful failures have brought you to the doorstep of *Manifesto 11.* Now, desperate times call for desperate measures. Sell! Sell! Sell! Sell everything! Sell your house! Sell your furniture! Sell any living thing attached to you or your house (so much for pet intimacy, but it's your fault)! Kiss your cat goodbye and whisper "bon voyage" to your fishys. Sell your stocks, socks, bonds, etc.! Sell your car and other means of transportation! Sell your identity (get rid of that social security number, credit cards, driver's license, etc.)! Sell anything that has not fallen under the aforementioned sellers! Then, and this is very important, give all the money you earned from the sales to your favorite charity. For example, the *Ellen Society* where women without tongues are the only members.

Even though one might think that there is no woman who would want a pathetic, worthless, penniless person like you, you know there is always some desperate woman who would find some value in you, especially a *RB* woman. So disappear! Move out of your state to a city with a large homeless population to which you can attach yourself. Or, isolate yourself: the Sahara Desert is said to be nice this time of year; and there is an ambassador's palace available in Texas as well as some nice, fenced-in, secured property in Montana.

Chapter 12

Consult Your *MAN* Index

This is your chance to thumb through information quickly to see where you stand with *RB* women. You *sensitive* males need to identify the food that you most associate yourself with and determine how you will fare with *RB* women. You are literally what you eat. Some of you are actually more than you eat and half of what you spill! So find your favorite food and see what the dating future holds for you:

➤ *BEEF.* Now here's a man's man. Shank, rump, round, tip, flank, T-bone, chuck, rib, or porterhouse—No Worries Mate! When you go up against *RB* women, you are ready. Real men don't eat quiche! You have old-fashioned western values. You are from a time when men were men and women stayed at home and did not vote. The rugged frontier was carved in your face and dirt from the range blasted a ring around the tub. You can handle anything that comes along, including *RB* women.

> *Greatest Skill:* Leaving up the toilet seat
> *Hobby:* Real men don't need no stinking
>   hobbies
> *Favorite Actor:* Arnold Schwarzenegger
> *Favorite Movie:* "The Terminator"

Proverb To Live By: "I'll be back"
Most Likeable About RB Women: Breasts

➢ *SALADS.* So you like roughage, huh? The roughage the better! Men who choose salads as their best food are a little on the hedonistic side. Not to the point of grunting "Me Tarzan, you Jane," but dominant nonetheless. When you bark out an order, you expect people to comply. *RB* women are no exception. They will have difficulty controlling or manipulating you unless you want to be controlled. Men who are in to salads do something because "It pleases me."—sort of the John Wayne approach to Old West relationships.

> *Greatest Skill:* Guzzling beer and puking at the same time
> *Hobby:* Underboss to the Godfather
> *Favorite Actor:* John Wayne (The Duke)
> *Favorite Movie:* "In Harms Way"
> *Proverb To Live By:* "Never hit a pilgrim"
> *Most Likeable About RB Women:* Hoofspah

➢ *VEGETABLES.* To the man who best likes vegetables presents a lifelong allegiance to his mother. The umbilical cord is not quite severed nor is it likely to be cut. You are a mamma's boy! Actually, this will work in your favor in dealing with a *RB* woman. Why? Because mamma must approve of her and anybody else who shows the slightest interest in their little boy. You know that mamma will seldom approve of anybody. Her son is too good for anybody and certainly *RB* women would be at the bottom of her list of acceptability. Mamma does not want her son to be taken away from her even legitimately. It would be very messy indeed to try to cut the emotional umbilical cord in the adult male. So, you are safe. You're unlikely to be perceived as participating any kind of relationship let alone an emotionally mature one. Mamma may allow you to date to avoid queries about your sexual orientation, but a long-term relationship will certainly be out of the question. Indeed, two's company and three's a crowd!

Greatest Skill: Dusting furniture
Hobby: Stamp or coin collecting
Favorite Actor: Mickey Rooney
Favorite Movie: "Andy Hardy Cleans House"
Proverb To Live By: "Let he who taketh the
plunge return it by Friday"
Most Likeable About RB Women: Being ordered
around like a little boy

➢ *POTATOES.* Hey, Mr. Potato Head! Yah, you with the funny glasses, big nose and hands coming out of the sides of your body. Yah, you! You are probably a single man and destined to stay that way. Not even *RB* women will be enticed to forge a relationship with you. It is unlikely that they will be attracted to you although you probably will have your staunch supporters. Having the personality of a potato head will likely keep you safe from all kinds of female predators, including *RB* women. But you never know. Some women prefer a spudding personality.

Greatest Skill: Making homemade French fries
Hobby: Blowing Nose
Favorite Actor: Phyllis Diller
Favorite Movie: "Private Navy of Sgt. O'Farrell"
Proverb To Live By: "Even Hugh Hefner was a virgin once"
Most Likeable About RB Women: Facial features

➢ *FRUIT.* Does teeter-totter mean anything to you? Men who like fruit do not know which way to go. Their bent is uncertain. They are prime meat, er, fruit for exploitation by *RB* women. Not knowing which way to go or being "on the fence" is much worse than making a decision and choosing a side. Being indecisive will be the death of you. You must become decisive and stand on your own two feet if you are to have any chance of avoiding the arms of the woman who assumes she is *Mrs. Right.*

Greatest Skill: Spreading compost
Hobby: Collecting Salt and Pepper Shakers
Favorite Actor: Tiny Tim
Favorite Movie: "Tip Toe Through the Tulips"
Proverb To Live By: "To be or not to be"
Most Likeable About RB Women: Not sure

➤ *ICE CREAM.* I scream! You scream! We all scream for ice cream! Takes you back a few years, doesn't it? The saying that seems appropriate is "If you can't lick them, join them." Men who choose ice cream as their utmost food think they are smooth, cool characters. Well, at least that is the persona they attempt to present. However, *RB* women seldom buy it. They know dips when they see them. You will eventually be uncovered for the cone head that you are. The chances of forging a relationship with a *RB* woman is pretty slim even if they only want you for dessert.

> *Greatest Skill:* Erecting cones for highway projects
> *Hobby:* Egg hunts
> *Favorite Actor:* Dan Aykroyd
> *Favorite Movie:* "Coneheads"
> *Proverb To Live By:* "Head off filibusters and always get to the point"
> *Most Likeable About RB Women:* Tops of their heads

➤ *FISH.* Is it I or is there something fishy here? In a word, fish smell; well, that was two words. Men who best associate themselves with fish have a built-in and protective aroma, if you will. It is kind of like the garlic thing only better (Italians typically favor the garlic approach). Women, in general, have a natural almost herbal tendency to avoid unflattering, smelly things, including smelly people.

It's kind of like being unkempt or sitting in a boys' locker room on the last day of school. Your choice of food provides a natural barrier that even *RB* women will need a strong desire or reason to traverse.

Greatest Skill: Passing gas or breaking wind
Hobby: Lighting matches in bathrooms
Favorite Actor: Don Knotts
Favorite Movie: "The Incredible Mr. Limpet"
Proverb To Live By: "Nip it, nip it, nip it right
　　　　　　　　　　　 in the bud"
Most Likeable About RB Women: Gills

➤ *CHICKEN.* The other, other white meat. Well, Chicken Little, your chosen food best describes the man. You're afraid to do anything. You're not a risk taker. Like blind sheep, you follow and step-in whatever is in front of you. You had little disregard for your parents' concern. Your mother queried in your youth, "If they jump off the side of a cliff, are you going to jump off the cliff too?" In response, you smirked as much as your facial bones would allow without discovery. Internally, you thought "yes," but were sure to say, "no" to your mother to avoid a well-planted slap across your face (for this now, we just shoot people). You are a highly suggestive individual that *RB* women have little difficulty in manipulating. You will do whatever they tell you to do because you are either too stupid or too scared to do otherwise.

Greatest Skill: Plucking chickens
Hobby: Tar and feathering
Favorite Actor: Eddie Haskel
Favorite Movie: "Leave it to Eddie's Father"
Proverb To Live By: "In a perilous emergency, a coward thinks with his legs"
Most Likeable About RB Women: Legs

➤ *HAM.* Well, this is certainly calling the kettle black! Ham is the food that best describes the man. Bob Hope and Bing Crosby use to argue with each other as to who was the greatest ham. And they really did ham it up, didn't they? A man who loves ham is a self-serving man (sort of rhymes, doesn't it?). He wants all the attention that the gods are willing to bestow and then some. What a perfect trap for the *RB* woman to exploit. Simply said, if you have a need, she fills the need. If you have two needs, she fills two needs. If you have three needs...I guess you get the point. You might as well order a pizza (see below)! You have no defenses and denial is not sufficiently important to consider. In other words, she's got you and you don't even care. How pitiful!

Greatest Skill: Stretching bacon so that it cooks straight
Hobby: Looking in the mirror
Favorite Actor: Gordy
Favorite Movie: "Gordy"
Proverb To Live By: "Between two evils, always pick the one you never tried"

Most Likeable About RB Women: Looking in
her mirror

➢ *PIZZA.* Beware! Warning! Where's Dr. Smith? A guy who loves pizza is the wimpiest man who is easily influenced. RB women will no doubt overwhelm him. Get a pizza! It requires no effort. You dial seven digits on the phone (maybe only one if you have it encoded on your speed dial, smuck). You don't even have to get off the couch. You have the pizza delivered to your door. How easy you are. You are a man that always takes the easy way out. You put no thought or effort in what you do. *A RB* woman will eat you alive even with anchovies!

Greatest Skill: Eating grapes from overhead
while laying on the couch
Hobby: Counting toppings on a pizza and
dividing them by its circumference
(estimate of pizza pi)
Favorite Actor: Dean Martin
Favorite Movie: "Like a Big Pizza Pie"
Proverb To Live By: "Never order an extra
anything in life because they
will forget to give it you"
Most Likeable About RB Women: Her delivery

Now that you have made your choice and charted your future destiny, let's see how well you did. Are you strong and able to counteract the wills and ways of *RB* women? Or are you a linguini, all shriveled and limp—

no match for your mamma let alone a *RB* gal. Are you man enough to find out? If you say so…

The *MAN* index is an indices that ranges from 10 to 100 (with a mean of 50 and standard deviation of 10 for those statistical people out there) where the greater the index, the more susceptible you are to the ways of the wicked *RB* woman.

The *MAN* index is presented graphically as follows:

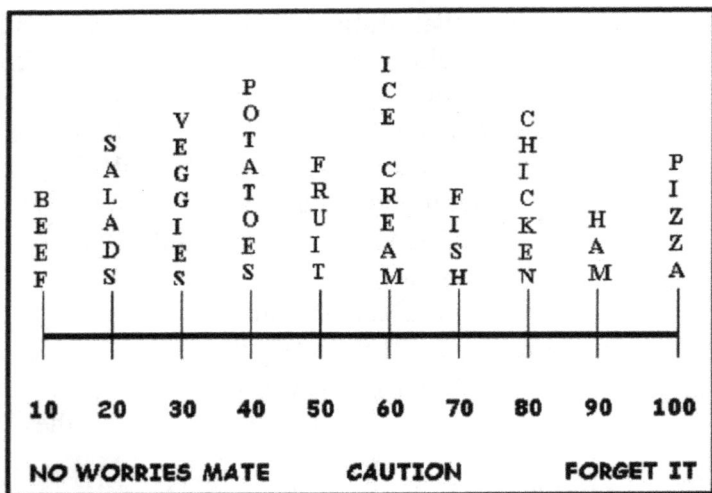

10	20	30	40	50	60	70	80	90	100
BEEF	SALADS	VEGGIES	POTATOES	FRUIT	ICE CREAM	FISH	CHICKEN	HAM	PIZZA

NO WORRIES MATE   CAUTION   FORGET IT

THE MAN INDEX: YOU ARE WHAT YOU EAT!

Chapter 13

Side-Stepping the Rules Manifestos at a Peep for Those Who Need Cliff Notes

For the discriminating reader who is either illiterate or does not have the time to read the book and cannot find this book on audiotapes, here are the *Side-Stepping Manifestos* at a peep:

Manifesto 1:	Shy Away From Women Who Show the Slightest Interest in You; Remember: Nobody Knows How You Really Feel!
Manifesto 2:	Avoid Eye Contact with Women and for Heaven's Sake...Shut Up!
Manifesto C:	Go Somewhere Else When She Tells You Where to Go
Manifesto 4:	Hep. 10 - 27 - 51 - Hike!
Manifesto E:	Divest Yourself of All Communicative Devices and Reduce the Odds of First Contact
Manifesto 6:	Avoid Women with CPMS
Manifesto G:	Remember, You're Not Just a Piece of Meat
Manifesto H:	A Dog is a Man's Best Friend

Chapter N

Glossary for Understanding Women in Cyberspace: Coping in the 21st Century

Will there really be any significant differences between men and women in the 21st century? Perhaps a poem may say it best:

Differences between us always were and will be,
Yet sameness is exhorted more now than ever.
Man and woman will soon enter the 21st century,
Different as can be, yet certainly no better.

What one has, the other wants
Although each also has what neither embraces.
Into the 21st century, sameness they will flaunt;
Even differences will have familiar faces.

So how will man and woman be chronicled?
More different or perhaps not?
The question is actually quite rhetorical,
For we began different more than not!
Viva la difference!

Advancing technology has brought us new terminology and a need for understanding this terminology if men are to be successful in coping with *RB* women in the 21st century. The following definitions are offered in addressing this need and to limit man's gullibility in Cyberspace in the next century:

Access Time
The period of time that elapses between a woman making eye contact with a man and said woman arriving at her intended destination.

Active Partition
The brain of a Cyberspace woman that contains her operating system that is loaded when eye contact is initially made.

Adapter
Anything that a woman uses to provider herself with added capabilities.

Address
Something that men want to avoid getting and giving away.

Algorithm
A formal set of instructions that women follow to perform a specific task and are operationalized once eye contact is established and the active partition set.

Alt Newsgroups
A cyber woman's diary that often contains controversial thoughts and experiences.

Antivirus Program
An application program that men run to avoid or eliminate viruses (e.g., the dreaded *Wedded Virus).*

Applet
A small application program limited in scope to one small but futile task (e.g., dating).

Arbitration
The set of rules used to manage a relationship when inquiries or requests are made by multiple users, i.e., men and women.

ASCII
Pronounced "askee." Acronym for *Avoid Sexual Contact with Infectious Idiots.* A standard interaction scheme whereby avoidance of such contact minimizes the "dumbing down" of society.

Asynchronous Transmission
Specifies the typical unequal communications transmitted between men and women, particularly *RB* women.

AT Command Set
A set of standard instructions used by women to activate the testosterone level in men to manipulate communications.

Attenuation
The decrease in power of signals transmitted by a woman during interchanges once she has a man's attention.

Autoexec. bat
A batch of things wanted by women every time they come into contact with men (e.g., wallet, credit cards, car, house keys, etc.).

Back-End Processor
Used by *RB* women when the direct approach fails.

Background Noise
Any unwanted signal from women as they attempt to initiate contact with men.

Backup
What men do who do poorly at applying the manifestos in this book.

Backward - Compatible
Men who have backed-up before.

Bad Track Table
The success rate of *RB* women in their quest to date any resemblance of a man.

Baud
A measure of speed that women use to determine how fast they are accomplishing their set tasks that lead to dating.

Benchmark
An established table that quantifies a woman's performance in luring men and allows for average comparisons of speed, reliability and accuracy.

Beta Software
Testing dating places for the first time.

Binary
Any scheme that uses two different states, components, conditions or conclusions (e.g., a *RB* woman and her mother).

BIOS
Pronounced "bye-os." Acronym for *Battle Interest in Opposite Sex.* A system that minimizes, delays or interferes with dating interests between men and women.

Bit
Used by women in their love potions as in a *bit* of this and a *bit of* that...

Boot
Often given to men before, during or after dating.

Browser
What men and women used to explore each other as it lets your interest wander without limitations, consequences or punishment.

Buffer
That which comes between men and women and arrests conditions leading beyond first contact.

Bug
A man or woman with 4 arms and 4 legs.

Bus
A big yellow thing.

Byte
Represents a very small amount and usually embarrassing to the holder.

Cache
Pronounced "cash." A method by which women improved their performance in snagging men and then take that cache to the bank.

Carpal-Tunnel Syndrome
A form of injury caused by holding hands during the dating process.

CD-ROM
Acronym for *Cheap bate - Ring Often Missing.* What a *RB* woman typically ends up with when she is willing to date anything that moves.

CMOS
Pronounced "c-moss." Acronym for *Can Men Outmoded Survive?* Recognizes that women have increasingly taken over the roles of men and it is just a matter of time before men become obsolete and extinct.

Cold Boot
Same as "Boot" (often given to men before, during or after dating) except that it occurs during the cold season of the year.

Crash
An unexpected halt in the dating process typically provoked by pushy men or women.

Decibel
A *RB* woman from the north who is one tenth of a southern belle.

Defragmentation
The process of reorganizing your life so that it appears to be continuous rather than filled with splinter events.

Device
Anything that a woman can use to manipulate, control or manage men.

Dip Switch
That which best describes *RB* women who go from one man to another.

Docking Station
That which occurs sometime during the dating process for men who are unable to successfully apply the manifestos in this book.

DOS
Part of the do-be-do-be-dos.

DOS Prompt
Visual confirmation for a woman who has made eye contact with a man and realizes that he is ready.

Dot Pitch
The increasingly squinting pattern of eyes during the dating process.

Download
The opposite of upload (see "upload").

Dynamic Link Library
Abbreviated *DLL* That which *RB* women attempt to *engage* and men attempt to avoid.

E-mail
E-mail is sent by men and Fe-mail is sent by women.

Emulator
Something that stands for something else but something you never understand because you never understood what is stood for in the first place.

Error
The difference between what was expected and what actually occurred (e.g., the outcome of a date).

Expansion Slot
Something you use to give you access to a bus or other means of transportation.

Fatal Error
An error from which there is no hope of recovery without strictly following the manifestos in this book.

Fax
Abbreviation for something that is a reasonable facsimile of something else.

File Allocation Table
Abbreviated FAT. Describes the eventual condition of a man or woman who has difficulty getting away from the [kitchen] table.

Floppy Disk
A flat, round, specially coated plastic disk enclosed in a protective jacket that is typically the contraceptive of choice of *RB* women.

Formatting
The process that women use on men so that men can be used by women.

Gigabyte
A person who giggles at a byte (a very small amount that is usually embarrassing to the holder).

Half-Height Drive
A small person that has very little motivation.

High Level Format
The process that *classy* women use on men so that can be used by *classy* women (see *formatting).*

Impedance
An electrical property of cable that unites capacitance, inductance and resistance—not to be confused with *impotence.*

Infection
The presence of a computer virus or a specific potential outcome of dating.

Interface
That point where a connection is made when men are unable to successfully apply the manifestos in this book.

Interrupt
A signal that is attempted by men who are coming under the grasp of *RB* women.

Joystick
A multidirectional pointing device where one or more fingers are used to get a point across.

Jumper
A method of choosing a single or multiple manifestos in this book to counteract the engaging nature of the opposite sex.

Kernel
The most fundamental structure in the armed forces that often remains hidden until needed.

Kilobyte
A person who is driven to murder because of a byte (a very small amount that is usually embarrassing to the holder).

Latency
The time that elapses between a request for data and started the data transfer; not to be confused with the *latency period* in psychosexual development of pre-adolescence.

Local Bus
The big yellow thing that serves your local community school.

Lost Chain
Once kept around a person's neck, something carelessly gobbled-up by that person who was sitting at the *FAT* table (see *File Allocation Table*).

Male Connector
A cable connector with pins designed to engage the sockets on the female part of the connector.

Mean Time Between Failures
Statistical average length of time betweens dates for men or women.

Megabyte
A person who no longer feels like a million because of a byte (a very small amount that is usually embarrassing to the holder).

Memory Chip
A chip off the old block under 640K.

MIDI
Pronounced "middy." Acronym for *My Intimate Date Interface*. Standard protocols used by men that they believe will lead to intimacy *via* synthesizers and musical instruments.

MS-DOS
An alias often used by *RB* women or *Mrs. Right* as they travel as a single woman.

Multitasking
The simultaneous execution of two or more manifestos in this book.

Nano
A taunting phrase often used by immature men or women as in "Nano, nano, nano…"

Nanosecond
Same as "nano" above, but said much faster.

Node
A neer, a female neer.

Non-interlaced
A woman who makes a single pass at a man to reduce unwanted flicker.

Null
A dull date; a zero; and therefore has no value.

Offline
A man or woman who is not in ready mode and is therefore unavailable for use.

Online
A man or woman who is in ready mode and available for use.

Parallel Port
Two towns having harbors that lie next to each other.

Parity
Something between men and women that does not occur beyond the dating process.

Petabyte
A person with a small pet that bytes.

Plug-and-Bug
Horse and buggy strategies of a by-gone era used by women to entrap men and play it back if necessary.

Power Surge
A brief but sudden increase in estrogen or testosterone levels that can be destructive during a dating relationship.

Protocol
The specification that defines the procedures to follow when women transmit and men receive information during first contact.

Protocol Stack
A woman who is more difficult to resist during protocol.

Queue
Pronounced "Q." An alien being in *Star Trek* episodes that is god-like and omnipotent.

RAM
Acronym for *Run Away Men* for those men who were not successful in applying the manifestos in this book.

Reboot
Same as "Boot" (often given to men before, during or after dating) and indicates that you were foolish enough to date the same woman twice.

ROM
Acronym for *Run Over Men* for those *RB* women who date men who were not successful in applying the manifestos in this book.

Scanner
An optical device subconsciously used by men each time they see a woman.

Seek Time
The length of time required for a men and women to find each other.

Serial Mouse
Rats that start their day with a hearty breakfast cereal.

Shareware
A form of distribution that makes people who were once married freely available on a trial basis to somebody else.

Stand Alone
What a *RB* woman hopes to avoid and the targeted male hopes to be.

Surge Suppressor
Any device, technique, medication or behavioral strategy that suppresses a power surge (A brief but sudden increase in estrogen or testosterone levels that can be destructive during a dating relationship).

Terminal
Describes a man who fails to apply successfully at least one of the manifestos in this book.

Track
One of many concentric rings in the brain of a *RB* woman that is believed responsible for their destiny to date anything that moves.

Upgrade
The process of applying more powerful strategies by *RB* women against those men who are successfully applying the manifestos in this book.

Upload
The opposite of download (see "download").

Vaccine
An application that removes and destroys unexpected side effects during the dating process.

Version Number
A method used by *RB* women to identify each of their preys.

Virtual Reality
The illusion that men often portray to demonstrate that they are really in control.

Wait State
Something that men find hard to do when they are at the whim of a *RB* woman.

Warm Boot
Same as "Boot" (often given to men before, during or after dating) except that it occurs during the warm season of the year.

Windows
A transparent object that most women can see through that men cannot due to the differences in their domestic proclivities.

Zero Wait State
A man with no wait state (see "Wait State").

About the Author

The interest, drive and motivation to become a writer often have their roots early in life even though one may not realize at the time. I was an 8-year-old third grader when I had some conscious awareness that writing is a good thing. It was then that several friends and I started a neighborhood newsletter.

With typewriter in hand, the newsletter was born and essentially shared much about nothing that went on in the neighborhood. However, our neighbors were kind enough to give us 25 cents for each newsletter... and most paying customers could actually read the carbon blur caused by a dozen carbon sheets.

As the years passed, I took several courses in writing and things didn't seem so blurry. I began writing little stories for children of friends and relatives that included their personal data about their personal lives. This happened about 15 years before such books became popular commercially. It was these stories that formed the basis of my first children's book, *Twelve Upon A Time ...*

I also wrote a mystery/adventure novel, *Mirror, Mirror at 1600 D.C.* This political intrigue novel gives you characters in believable relationships bound up in a mystery and an adventure that will keep you speculating throughout the book.

After that serious effort, I took a lighthearted

approach in this parody book, *Side-Stepping the Rules: Broken or Not.* This parody provides the reader with the gift of laughter from the male perspective as it offers men childish ways for escaping the clutches of the woman who thinks she is Mrs. Right.

Side-Stepping the Rules: Broken or Not provides the sensitive male with 11 manifestos that will serve as countermeasures to the wiles of RB women. No worries mate! Even if you are unsuccessful with the first 10 manifestos, the final manifesto, "Sell your house and blend invisibly with the homeless," still provides you—the most pitiful representation of mankind—a way out.

As with all my books, I hope the reader enjoys the read as much as I enjoyed the write.

Other Books by the Author
Published by CCB Publishing

Mirror, Mirror at 1600 D.C.
ISBN 978-0-9810246-1-5

The role of the Presidency is complicated more than enough for Elizabeth Ashton without the added political burden of being the first woman elected to this high office in America. She is delighting her supporters and converting readily her critics when she is kidnapped while attending a fundraiser. The unfolding plot is a matter of survival—not only personal survival, but also hanging in the balance is the endurance of the Presidency and democracy in America. The missing President must be recovered—dead or alive.

Beginnings
ISBN 978-1-926585-10-9

Beginnings is based on the lives of Greg and Charly that propels the reader on an emotional roller coaster, as events unfold in their lives, including the more absurd and humorous aspects of life. *Beginnings* traverses the singledom lives of Greg and Charly and bring them together. The global benchmarks that help define them and a people unfold for each decade of their lives. We all encounter collectively many beginnings and beginnings of the end. We share them for they are part of what we call the human condition. Greg and Charly experience many beginnings and beginnings of the end—some predictable, some unexpected. Some beginnings are critical moments in our lives as they forever change us for better or worse—they bring us together or tear us apart. They are intimately tied to human relationships as they strengthen or weaken the stuff that binds us. The beginnings that impact on Greg and Charly unfold in the pages to come. Yet, these are not necessarily unique experiences and readers will relate to their own beginnings and beginnings of the end. However, I am getting ahead of myself. I would like to tell about the circumstances of my world just before my beginning and the woman of my life, Charly . . .

Twelve Upon A Time...
ISBN 978-1-926585-69-7

Twelve Upon A Time... is a storybook for families. Each monthly story is illustrated by the original drawings of children whose interpretation of the only be seen through their eyes. The stories are written to assist the imagination of children and to strengthen the parent and child bond through the sharing of heart-warming, silly, absurd and believably impossible tales.

A sample of chapters:

January: Bronto's Visitors from Another Time follows the adventures of a family   back to the time of prehistoric dinosaurs and their search for the time portal that   began their misadventure on New Year's

Eve.

April: The Great Festival of Rabbunia follows the adventures of children to the mythical land of Rabbunia where they celebrate the Great Festival with the inhabitants of Rabbunia.

August: The "Yad Gnihton Taerg"on the Mirror Planet celebrates the "Yad Gnihton Taerg" on the mirror planet Tenalp in the central city of Rorrim, a celebration that occurs just once every 500 years.

November: 'Twas the Night Before Thanksgiving... is a Thanksgiving story that unfolds in rhyme while children wait for a visit from Ninja Turkey!